# Just One Careless Moment

# Just One Careless Moment

## Seven Days of Noticing What Matters

*Because a single pause has the power to unravel—or make whole—everything.*

Holli Bradish-Lane

*Sometimes the smallest shift holds the greatest power.*
*— A whisper, a pause, a single breath.*

# Contents

These reflections came during a pause.

I stepped away from familiar rhythms and into a different pace.
A different landscape.
A place where attention widened simply by slowing down.

Rest was not scheduled.
Listening was not planned.
Stillness arrived on its own time.

As the days unfolded, something subtle began to surface.
How much meaning lives in moments that pass too quickly to be noticed.
How easily care slips when movement outpaces awareness.
How much becomes visible when space is allowed.

The seven days that follow emerged from that quiet.
Not as conclusions, but as observations gathered slowly.
Each one shaped by presence returning, moment by moment.

This book is an invitation into that same posture.
To move more gently through the pages.
To linger.
To listen.

What appears small often carries more weight than expected.
And a single moment, held with care, can quietly shape what comes next.

# Introduction

I gave myself permission to step away.
To rest. To recharge. To remember what stillness feels like.

We traveled south from home in Colorado into New Mexico.
A short distance on a map, and a distinct shift in pace and texture.
The light settles differently there.
Colors deepen.
The landscape opens.
The air carries a sense of age and patience.

An enchanted place.

One stop brought us to an *Earthship*, a self-sustaining home designed decades ago with simple intention.
To preserve the Earth.
To tread lightly.
To live in harmony with what has already been given.

That intention stayed with me.

Because in our lives, in our relationships, in the patterns we move through each day, attention thins as momentum builds.

Movement quickens.
Moments pass without being held.

Change often arrives quietly.
Through small shifts that carry more weight than expected.
Through a pause missed.
Through a word spoken without care.

Sometimes, it comes down to
one careless moment.

This series grew from noticing those moments.

It is an invitation to awareness.
To slowing.
To returning to presence.

To remembering that what seems small can shape what follows.

# Day 1: One careless moment.

*"To live awake is to honor the fragile power of each passing second."*

That's all it takes.
A split-second distraction behind the wheel.
A word spoken in anger you can't take back.
A misstep on a trail you've walked a hundred times.
A decision made in haste, without listening to your gut.

It's unsettling how fragile things can be—relationships, bodies, trust, peace.
How easily the fabric of a life can shift from steady to unraveling.
Not out of recklessness, but out of assumption.
Familiarity. Auto-pilot.

This isn't about living in fear.
It's about living *awake*.
With reverence. With responsibility. With a sense that every moment matters more than we often let it.

Because one careless moment can change everything.
But so can one mindful one.

**Reflect:**

- When was the last time you noticed yourself on autopilot?

- What does *living awake* look like for you right now?

# Day 2: One careless moment... and the silence begins.

*"We shape our days by what we notice. What we miss. What we hold with care."*

Not the peaceful kind—
The kind that creeps in after something's been broken.
A silence made of things unsaid, of glances avoided,
Of hearts retreating just enough to feel the gap.

It settles into routines.

Into rooms still shared.

Into conversations that skim the surface and move on.

Life keeps moving.

So do we. Just slightly farther apart each day.

It doesn't always roar.
Sometimes it just *drifts in.*
Soft. Unnoticed.
Until one day, it's all that's left.

**Reflect:**

- Where has silence crept in—between you and someone you care about?

- Is there something left unsaid that's quietly asking for a voice?

# Day 3: One careless moment... and trust slips.

*"May we learn to notice before we break, breathe before we speak, and soften before we shut down."*

You didn't mean to forget.
Or dismiss.
Or joke when you should've listened.

But the heart you were holding noticed.
And suddenly, the solid ground beneath your connection
Feels a little less certain.

Trust is built in layers—
but chipped away in shards.

It isn't the moment itself.
It's the pause that follows.
The question that lingers unasked.
The sense that something shifted, quietly.

**Reflect:**

- When have you unintentionally chipped away at trust—with someone else or with yourself?

- What might it look like to begin rebuilding that trust, one layer at a time?

# Day 4: One careless moment... and the mirror changes.

*"Be careful how you speak to yourself. You are always listening."— Maya Angelou*

You said something to yourself that you'd *never* say to a friend.
You looked in the mirror and saw only flaws.
You believed a lie that you're not enough—again.

And even though it was just a flicker,
it carved a little deeper into your reflection.

The mirror learns from repetition.
From tone.
From the way meaning settles before thought can intervene.
What begins as a whisper becomes a posture.
A stance you carry forward.
A story the body starts to believe.

Words, even internal ones, have weight.
Be careful what you tell the person you see every day.

**Reflect:**

- What is one thing you said to yourself this week that you would never say to a friend?

- What would compassion sound like in your own voice?

# Day 5: One careless moment... and your breath forgets you.

*"Your body remembers what your mind forgets. Start with a breath."*

You're rushing. Reacting.
Answering before hearing.
Moving without feeling your feet on the ground.

And you don't even notice—you haven't exhaled in minutes.

Your shoulders inch higher.
Your jaw tightens without asking permission.
Time narrows.
The world speeds up.
All while your breath stands by, steady, patient.

Your body keeps the score.
Your breath remembers stillness.
It's waiting for you to come back.

Come back.

**Reflect:**

- When did you last truly feel grounded in your body?

- How does it feel to pause and *notice* your breath right now?

# Day 6: One careless moment... and the door closes.

*"Life changes in a moment. Not always loudly.
Sometimes quietly—beautifully."*

Not slammed. Just slowly… gently… shut.
An opportunity missed.
A kindness unspoken.
A reconnection left to "someday."

Time has a way of deciding for us.
Not out of cruelty.
Out of movement.
Moments keep going.
Lives keep unfolding.
And openings quietly complete their arc.

We think life gives second chances. Sometimes it does.
But not always.

The door doesn't always lock—
but it won't stay open forever.

**Reflect:**

- Is there a door you assumed would always be open?

- What does it mean to you to honor an opportunity while it's still available?

# Day 7: One careless moment... and grace arrives.

*"Grace isn't loud. It meets us in the space between regret and renewal."*

Yes, sometimes we stumble.
Say the wrong thing.
Forget what matters.
Fall short.

But grace—quiet, patient, and unbound—
waits to meet us there.

Not with judgment, but with a whisper:
*Begin again.*

Grace moves at the pace of honesty.
It meets willingness with warmth.
It steadies what has been shaken.
Restores dignity to the next step.
Opens space for choice.
Invites life to continue, shaped with care.

Because if one careless moment can change everything—
so can one *forgiving* one.


**Reflect:**

- Where in your life are you being invited to offer grace—to yourself or someone else?

- What would it feel like to begin again?

# Day 8: The Integration

*"Awareness without integration is like seeds never planted."*

Over the last seven days, we paused.
We held space for the small, nearly invisible pivots that shape a life.

We named the silence.
The slip.
The breath forgotten.
The door quietly closing.
And, finally, grace.

This wasn't about guilt.
It was about awareness.
An invitation to stop rushing long enough to see the weight of a whisper…
the turning of a thought…
the beauty of a second chance.

I began this series in the quiet of a retreat.
Rooted in an Earthship, where everything is designed to preserve rather than consume.
To restore balance rather than disrupt it.

That same wisdom belongs in our inner lives.
In how we move once noticing has begun.
In what we choose to carry forward.

Today is a moment to integrate.

Because awareness without integration is like seeds never planted.

So take a breath.
Take your time.
And plant something.

**What comes next will continue the work.**

**Reflect:**

- Which day of this series spoke to you the most?

- Why? What small shift will you carry into what follows?

# Re-entry

I returned home to Colorado carrying less than I left with.

No souvenirs. No answers neatly packaged. Just a quieter body and a mind that moved without rushing to fill space.

The landscape hadn't changed. The same foothills rose in familiar angles. The same light hit the Arkansas River in its late-afternoon way. But something in me moved differently through it.

Re-entry is rarely loud.
It happens in small recognitions.

The way conversation feels faster than necessary.
The way schedules reassert themselves without asking.
The way the body remembers stillness even as the calendar does not.

I noticed how quickly momentum tries to reclaim its place. Training plans. Writing deadlines.
Responsibilities that had waited patiently, now stepping forward again.

Nothing was wrong.
Nothing was urgent.

And that, perhaps, was the most unfamiliar sensation of all.

During the eight days away, listening had become the work. Back home, listening had to be chosen.

I found myself pausing before responding. Standing longer at windows. Letting silence finish its own sentences.

Not because I was trying to preserve the retreat.

But because something in me had shifted its center of gravity.

Life did not slow down to meet me.
I had to learn how to move without abandoning myself.

This was not the end of the stillness.
It was the beginning of carrying it.

Work continued. Writing moved into the world. What I had made quietly found its readers.

**There was no sense of arrival. Just the ongoing work of living.** What follows unfolded within less than four months.
A single season carried it.

# What Followed

### Glimpse 1 — Diagnosis

It began as something small.

A spot on his temple.
Easy to overlook. Easy to explain away.
The kind of thing life absorbs without pause.

We had been together for more than twenty-five years.
Long enough to recognize each other's rhythms. Long
enough to know when something shifts beneath the
surface, even before it has a name.

The word arrived quietly.
Melanoma.

It landed without drama and without permission.
Suddenly, the future felt less assumed. Time narrowed.
Ordinary moments carried more weight than they had
the day before.

I noticed how quickly the mind reached ahead.
Questions surfaced uninvited. How much time? How
much change? How much of what we imagined still fit?

He moved through it with steadiness. I moved through
it with attention. Watching. Listening. Holding the
space between what we knew and what we could not
yet know.

The days that followed were filled with small acts of care. Conversations slowed. Touch lingered longer than usual. We learned how to sit together without answers.

What surprised me most was not fear.
It was clarity.

Life sharpened. Presence deepened. The unimportant loosened its grip.

Awareness did not soften the reality.
It made it more honest.

## Glimpse 2 — Surgery

Waiting rooms slow everything.

Chairs line the walls. Voices stay low. Time loosens its grip on sequence. Careful work happens elsewhere, out of sight.

**I sat there alone.**

Acutely aware of the singularity of waiting while another body is held by unseen hands.

Surgery moves with precision.
Measured. Deliberate.
A body examined closely, layer by layer.

The spot was removed. Margins addressed. Deeper involvement noted. The lymph nodes, when examined, showed no spread. Enough clarity to proceed. Enough uncertainty to remain attentive.

There was no clean sense of "finished."
Only continuation.

The incision was extensive. A long series of careful lines, more akin to a reconstructive lift than a simple removal. A large section of skin taken. The body bearing visible evidence of what had been addressed. Healing would take time.

What followed required commitment rather than urgency. Months of immunotherapy. Ongoing care. A longer horizon than either of us had expected when the spot first appeared.

We returned home carrying a new rhythm.
Appointments. Monitoring. Attention sustained over time.

Life did not simplify.
It reorganized.

And we learned how to stand inside that reordering without rushing it forward.


## Glimpse 3 — Training

Training for an Ironman had been part of life for months.

Since the previous autumn, movement shaped the days. Early mornings. Repeated routes. Long hours built quietly, one after another. The body learned what was expected and responded with steadiness.

That rhythm held, even as other uncertainties entered the days.

After the diagnosis, schedules shifted. Effort adjusted. Some days shortened. Others softened. Training did not disappear, but it changed how it lived inside the day.

Stress registered differently now. Not as urgency, but as weight. Mortality moved closer to the surface, not announced, just present.

Faith stayed close.

The movement of running became a way to remain oriented. Breath after breath. Step after step. Training offered structure when the future felt less defined. It asked for attention without demanding answers.

The work continued without urgency. Just enough effort to linger inside the body, listening.

Training no longer pointed only toward a finish line. It pointed toward steadiness.

## Glimpse 4 — The Fall

The run was part of a familiar sequence.

Bike. Run. Bike again.

A pattern practiced many times before. Legs already warm. Attention settled into rhythm. The body knew what came next.

I was near the end of the run, moving easily through a section I had crossed countless times. A narrow bridge made of railroad ties. A small span. Nothing new to negotiate.

The foot landed wrong.

There was no chance to correct it. The body pitched forward and met the ground hard. Hands out, instinctual. Wrist taking the force. The sound of impact arriving before thought.

When I looked down, my hand was bleeding. Railroad-tie splinters were embedded across the palm and fingers. Some were long enough to catch and hold.

The wrist had changed, too. Not an ache. A clear disruption. Ligaments impacted. The hand no longer reliable for grip.

I got up carefully, working with what I had. Walked back to my bike. Mounted with one hand doing most of the work. Rode the seven miles back to my truck without the usual ease, the injured hand reduced to a careful participant.

The session closed itself without ceremony.

Later, the meaning of the fall gathered. Quietly. With clarity that did not rush.

Months of preparation had been interrupted in *a single moment*. Not by fatigue. Not by overuse. Just a misstep on familiar ground.

I listened.

And allowed the season ahead to change shape.


### Glimpse 5 — The Decision

The race loomed close.

Weeks, not months.
No meaningful window for healing.
The hand remained compromised, unreliable for the demands ahead.

And there was more in the field.

Ongoing cancer care shaped the days now. Appointments. Treatments. Attention required elsewhere. Energy allocated deliberately. What mattered most had already declared itself.

The question narrowed quickly.

Not whether training could continue.
Not whether endurance had been built.

But what care required now.

The body had spoken clearly.
The season had shifted.
Responsibility reordered itself.

There was no dramatic moment of choosing.
Just a pivot.

The race would not happen.

Not as sacrifice.
As alignment.

Care moved where it was needed. Toward healing that had no timetable. Toward partnership. Toward faith practiced daily rather than named.

Some paths close because another must be tended.

And so I turned toward what was already asking for my attention.

## Glimpse 6 — What Carries Forward

Time widened again.

Not because circumstances eased, but because attention had learned a different pace. What once rushed ahead now arrived one moment at a time.

Prayer changed shape.

Less about outcome.
More about orientation.
How to remain aligned when momentum pulls forward faster than wisdom.

Life did not return to what it had been.
It reorganized.

Care took precedence. Healing moved on its own timetable. Partnership asked for presence more than answers. Faith was no longer something spoken aloud so much as something lived inside the days.

Looking back, the pattern becomes visible.

Less than one hundred and twenty days carried it.

I was not reckless.
I was elsewhere.

The body knew how to keep moving.
The mind was still carrying what had not yet settled.

In **one careless moment**, the body interrupted the
story I had been telling myself about what comes next.

Not to punish.
Not to stop everything.

To redirect attention.

Some decisions are not endings.
They are acts of care.

What followed was not a return to certainty, but a
deeper steadiness. A willingness to listen more closely.
To trust what unfolds when presence leads.

That is what the eight days offered.
Not protection from life.
But a way to meet it awake.

And that, I have learned, is enough.

# Shalom

A gathering into wholeness.
A settling into safety.
The quiet knowing that what matters most is held
together.

As you step back into your days, may this blessing
travel with you.

May the Lord bless you and keep you.
May the Lord make His face shine upon you and be
gracious to you.
May the Lord turn His face toward you and grant you
shalom.

## About the Author

Holli Bradish-Lane writes at the intersection of presence and resilience. She is drawn to the quiet moments that shape a life long before we notice they matter.

Her work is rooted in lived experience—slowing down enough to listen, learning to notice the small internal shifts that precede change, and honoring the body as a keeper of wisdom. She lives off-grid on a 40-acre ranch, where nature, stillness, and deliberate rhythm inform both her writing and her work with others.

Professionally, Holli has spent over two decades in healthcare leadership, quality, patient safety, and performance improvement. She is a licensed respiratory therapist and certified health coach, and a pioneer in DNA-based health and metabolic coaching. Her approach blends science with deep attention to regulation, awareness, and integration—guiding individuals toward lasting, embodied well-being.

Above all, Holli is a storyteller and a companion in the work of living awake.

To learn more or connect, visit www.ironcruciblehealth.com

www.ingramcontent.com/pod-product-compliance
Lightning Source LLC
Chambersburg PA
CBHW051650120626
46551CB00015B/2297